All About
CLOUDS

Elise Wallace

Consultants

**Dr. Aaron O'Dea, Dr. Erin Dillon,
Dr. Natasha Hinojosa, and
Dr. Kimberly García-Méndez**
Researchers
Smithsonian Tropical Research Institute

Cheryl Lane, M.Ed.
Seventh Grade Science Teacher
Chino Valley Unified School District

Michelle Wertman, M.S.Ed.
Literacy Specialist
New York City Public Schools

Publishing Credits

Rachelle Cracchiolo, M.S.Ed., *Publisher*
Emily R. Smith, M.A.Ed., *SVP of Content Development*
Véronique Bos, *VP of Creative*
Dani Neiley, *Editor*
Fabiola Sepulveda, *Art Director*

Smithsonian Enterprises

Avery Naughton, *Licensing Coordinator*
Paige Towler, *Editorial Lead*
Jill Corcoran, *Senior Director, Licensed Publishing*
Brigid Ferraro, *Vice President of New Business and Licensing*
Carol LeBlanc, *President*

Image Credits: p.19 (right) Famartin; p.21 (bottom) Nichalp; p.22 NASA ID: as11-36-5299; p.27 NASA ID: PIA22424/NASA/JPL-Caltech/SwRI/MSSS/Gerald Eichstad/Sean Doran; all other images from Shutterstock and/or iStock or in the public domain

Library of Congress Cataloging in Publication Control Number:
2024039594

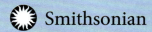

© 2025 Smithsonian Institution. The name "Smithsonian" and the Smithsonian logo are registered trademarks owned by the Smithsonian Institution.

This book may not be reproduced or distributed in any way without prior written consent from the publisher.

5482 Argosy Avenue
Huntington Beach, CA 92649
www.tcmpub.com
ISBN 979-8-7659-6894-9
© 2025 Teacher Created Materials, Inc.
Printed by: 51497
Printed in: China

Table of Contents

Captivating Clouds 4

The Basics of Cloud Formation. 6

Classifying Clouds 12

Weather Around the World 22

Our Cloudy Planet. 26

STEAM Challenge 28

Glossary. 30

Index. 31

Career Advice 32

Captivating Clouds

Floating feathers, gigantic puffballs, and misty stripes—clouds are shape-shifting marvels. Some clouds, such as stormy cumulonimbus, are legendary. Others, such as rainbow-colored nacreous clouds, are surprising and rare. Earth's skies are full of these wonders.

So, what exactly are clouds? Though clouds may look like fluffy cotton balls, they are actually made up of millions of itty-bitty water droplets. Clouds can also be made of tiny ice crystals or a mixture of ice crystals and water droplets. This may seem simple, but how, why, and where clouds form is a complex process.

Cloud formation relies on many factors. For starters, evaporation and condensation are key parts of cloud creation. Evaporation happens when water changes from a liquid to a gas. Condensation happens when water changes from a gas to a liquid. Temperature, **air pressure**, and region also affect how clouds form.

Clouds shape all kinds of weather around the world, and certain cloud types are more likely to appear in certain regions. For example, China is prone to storms called *typhoons*. Oklahoma and Texas are famous for their storms called *tornadoes*. Both of these severe weather events involve clouds.

Unraveling the mystery of why clouds do what they do is a fascinating journey. Let's take to the skies and learn all about clouds!

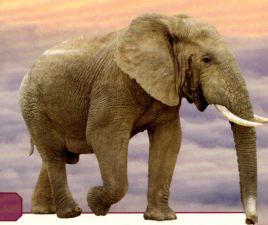

FUN FACT

Clouds can be enormously heavy. They can weigh about 500,000 kilograms (1.1 million pounds). That's about as much as 100 African elephants weigh!

The Basics of Cloud Formation

Cloud formation relies on water and evaporation. Across the planet, water is constantly evaporating. Water evaporates from places like streams, lakes, and oceans. Water can also evaporate from the leaves of plants through a process called *transpiration*. When water evaporates, the air becomes filled with an invisible gas called *water vapor*. Water vapor that **condenses** high in the sky becomes clouds.

Let's look closer at how water changes from an invisible gas to visible water droplets. As more water evaporates, more water vapor fills the air. Over time, the air becomes saturated. This means that the air cannot hold any more water vapor. The water molecules in the vapor need to condense and turn into water droplets.

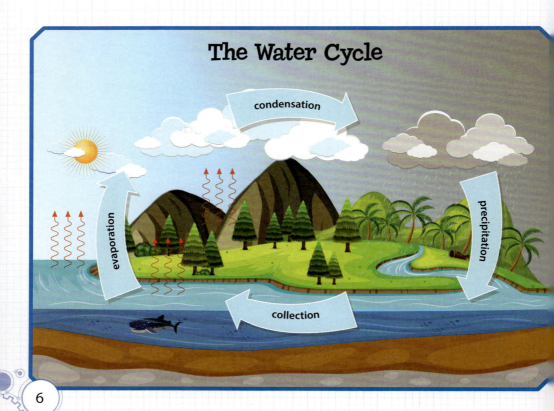

However, to become droplets, the water molecules must find a surface to latch onto. But these molecules have a hard time bonding to each other. This is where cloud condensation nuclei come in. These are teeny-tiny particles that are also called *cloud seeds*. Water molecules bond to these particles. Cloud condensation nuclei can be smoke, dust, dirt, and even salt from oceans.

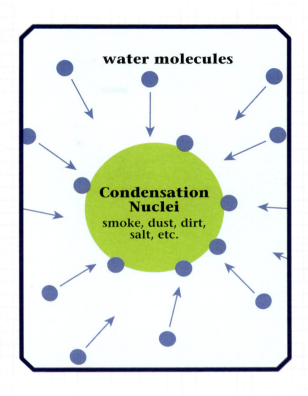

These particles make up very small parts of water droplets. Each is about one hundredth the size of a full droplet.

Near the ground, we see droplets as **dew**, **mist**, and **fog**. High in the air, we see these droplets as clouds.

Temperature and Air Pressure

Environmental factors, such as temperature and air pressure, can affect how clouds form. These forces aren't stable. They change constantly. This is why clouds can rapidly form, grow, and **dissipate**.

At 30 percent relative humidity, temperatures and dew point decrease as altitude increases.

1,820 meters
Temperature: 20 °C   Dew Point: 1.9 °C

914 meters
Temperature: 24 °C   Dew Point: 5.3 °C

Surface
Temperature: 33 °C Dew Point: 13.1 °C

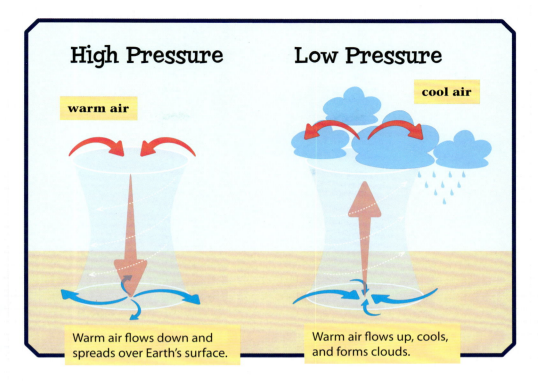

   Temperature plays a key part in cloud formation. The air's temperature dictates how much water vapor the air can hold. Warm air can hold more water vapor than cool air. Plus, warm air is lighter than cool air. This helps warm air rise. As moist, warm air rises, it begins to cool slightly. That's because temperatures drop as altitude, or height from the ground, increases. Clouds begin to form when air is cooled to its dew point. The dew point is the temperature at which air is saturated with water vapor. Dew points vary depending on location and air pressure.

   Air pressure is the total weight of the air around us, and it also affects cloud formation. Air pressure is either high or low. Just like temperature, air pressure drops as altitude increases. When air pressure is low, water vapor can expand. This causes it to cool and condense. So, low air pressure leads to water condensation and cloud formation. Areas that experience low air pressure usually have more clouds and storms. Meanwhile, areas that experience high air pressure usually have mild weather.

Rising Air

Cloud formation happens when air rises through the atmosphere. There are several ways that air can rise. The first way is through the heating of the ground by **solar energy**. As the sun heats the ground, water evaporates, creating moist, warm air. This warm air rises. As it rises, temperature and air pressure drop, making the water vapor condense and form clouds.

Another way rising air occurs is when wind comes into contact with a landform, such as a hill or mountain. When wind blows against a landform, it is forced upward. As the wind rises, it cools down and then condenses.

Air also rises when two sources of wind that are blowing from different directions come together. This is called a *convergence*. During a convergence, some air can be forced upward. This rising air results in condensation. Air also rises during **turbulence**. Turbulence happens when air moves in a way that is surprising, such as a sudden increase in speed.

Lastly, **weather fronts** can cause air to rise and condense. Fronts happen in different ways, but generally, they occur near the ground between two different **air masses**. For example, during a warm front, a warm air mass moves over a cold air mass. This warm air rises, cools, and condenses. During a cold front, a dense and cold air mass will force a warm air mass upward, resulting in clouds.

Atmospheric Fronts

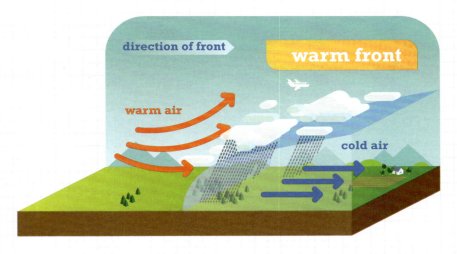

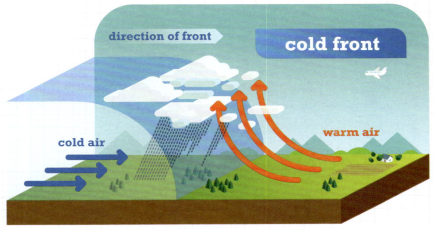

Classifying Clouds

Staring up at the sky, it may seem like there are a million different kinds of clouds! Scientists have designed **classifications** that help people identify and name the clouds they see. Mainly, clouds are grouped by how they look and at what heights they appear in the sky.

In 1803, a chemist named Luke Howard was fascinated with **meteorology**. He created the first classification of clouds in a published essay. Howard grouped clouds into three main categories: cirrus, stratus, and cumulus. Scientists continue to use these core cloud categories.

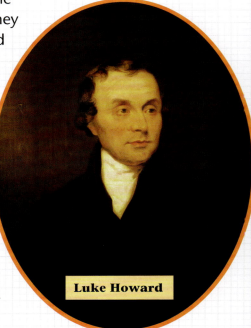

Luke Howard

MATHEMATICS

Measuring Clouds

Cloud cover is measured in a unit called *oktas* that divides the sky into eight equal parts. For example, if the sky is completely clear, a rating of zero oktas is given. If the sky is covered in clouds, a rating of eight oktas is given. Nine oktas is used for instances when the sky can't be seen due to fog. Take a look at the sky today. How would you describe it, using oktas?

CLOUD COVER

Symbol	Rating (in oktas)	
○	0	sky fully clear
◐	1	
◔	2	
◑	3	
◐	4	sky half cloudy
◕	5	
◕	6	
◕	7	
●	8	sky fully cloudy
⊗	9	sky obstructed from view

Core Cloud Types

Cirrus clouds are wispy, feathery clouds that occur at high altitudes. These clouds are made up of ice crystals and often appear in patchy groups or long stripes. In Latin, *cirrus* means "lock of hair"—the perfect name for these hairlike clouds. At sunrise and sunset, you might see cirrus clouds glowing yellow and red. These clouds are the sign of an approaching warm front.

cirrus clouds

The next core cloud category is stratus. In Latin, the word *stratus* means "flattened or spread out." Stratus clouds are gray, shapeless, and broad. They provide a lot of cloud cover, often blanketing the sky. They are low-altitude clouds that develop when air moves parallel to the ground. When stratus clouds form very close to the ground, they take the shape of mist or fog.

stratus clouds

Cumulus, the third category, might be the most famous clouds. These are the white, cotton ball-like clouds that many people think of when they imagine clouds. Cumulus clouds have clearly defined edges. They are typically flat on the bottom and puffy on top, similar to a head of cauliflower. The flat bases of cumulus clouds mark the altitude at which water vapor has condensed into water droplets. Cumulus clouds form in a range of sizes, from fairly small to super giant. They are usually associated with sunny weather.

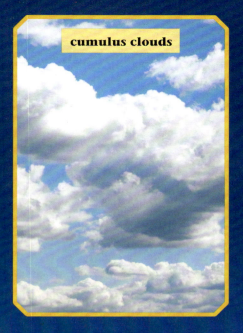

cumulus clouds

Like stratus clouds, cumulus clouds form at low altitudes. However, unlike stratus clouds, cumulus clouds form when air moves vertically rather than horizontally. Air has to move up from the ground for these clouds to form.

ARTS

Cloud Gate

Clouds have been the subject of many famous works of art. In Chicago, you can find one of the world's most impressive cloud tributes: Cloud Gate. (Due to its shape, people have nicknamed it "The Bean.") Imagined and designed by Anish Kapoor, Cloud Gate is a gigantic, stainless steel sculpture that reflects the city, its people, and the sky above.

15

Ten Cloud Types

Today, scientists use an expanded form of Luke Howard's system to classify clouds. It is called the *International Cloud Atlas*. The atlas includes Howard's original cloud types: cumulus, stratus, and cirrus. It also includes seven other cloud types, bringing the total to ten. Many of the new cloud categories are combinations of Howard's cloud types. For example, the atlas includes a cloud type called *cirrostratus*. This is a combination of Howard's cirrus and stratus clouds.

The ten types of clouds are ordered by their altitudes. The atlas lists high-level, mid-level, and low-level clouds. The three types of clouds are found at different altitudes depending on their location in the world.

16

High-Level Clouds

The three types of high-level clouds are cirrus, cirrocumulus, and cirrostratus. Like cirrus clouds, cirrocumulus and cirrostratus clouds are made of tiny ice crystals.

When cirrus clouds encounter turbulent winds, cirrocumulus clouds form. Contrails, or condensed water vapor trails created by airplanes, can also form cirrocumulus clouds. Cirrocumulus clouds appear grainy. They look like pebbles of white sand dotting the sky. Meanwhile, cirrostratus clouds are **translucent** and smooth. They might look like a blanket of sheer silk stretched across the sky. These clouds form when cirrus clouds thicken as a warm front approaches. Cirrostratus clouds can be a sign that rain is on the way.

cirrus clouds

cirrocumulus clouds

cirrostratus clouds

17

Mid-Level Clouds

There are three types of mid-level clouds. Their names are altocumulus, altostratus, and nimbostratus.

Altocumulus clouds are white and grey. They are made of both water droplets and ice crystals. These clouds can take on many shapes. They can appear small and patchy or provide layered cloud cover. Patchy altocumulus clouds are called *cloudlets*.

altocumulus clouds

altostratus clouds

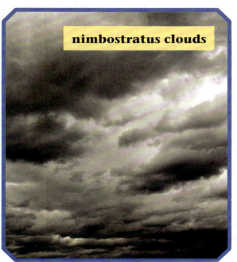
nimbostratus clouds

When cirrostratus clouds lower, they can form altostratus clouds. Altostratus clouds are often gray and translucent. They blanket the sky with thin, shapeless cloud cover. They are often too thin to blot out the sun's rays. When altostratus clouds begin to dissipate, they can form altocumulus clouds.

Warm fronts can cause altostratus to become even denser, resulting in nimbostratus clouds. These are dense rain clouds. The term *nimbo* comes from the Latin word *nimbus*, which means "rainy cloud." The sun's rays often can't be seen through the thick, gray cloud clover of nimbostratus clouds.

SCIENCE

Clouds and Temperatures

Clouds affect temperatures on Earth. During the day, clouds close to Earth's surface can block out heat from the sun. This makes temperatures on Earth cooler. Meanwhile, at night, higher clouds can trap heat in the atmosphere. This makes temperatures on Earth warmer.

Low-Level Clouds

There are four types of low-level clouds. Two have been discussed already: cumulus and stratus clouds. The other two types of low-level clouds are cumulonimbus and stratocumulus.

Cumulonimbus clouds are huge, anvil-shaped clouds that develop from cumulus clouds. These giant storm clouds cause severe weather. They can create tornadoes, lightning storms, and heavy rain.

cumulonimbus clouds

When stratus clouds break apart, they often form stratocumulus clouds. These clouds tend to be puffy, round, and arranged in groups or lines. They can also ripple gracefully across the sky like waves.

stratocumulus clouds

Rare Clouds

There are ten main types of clouds, but there are also many others! Some of the other cloud types are very rare. Lenticular clouds are one example. They are often made up of layered, round shapes. They can look like floating tornadoes, flying saucers, or camera lenses. Lenticular clouds get their name because of their lens-like shape.

lenticular clouds

Another rare cloud type is altocumulus castellanus. In Latin, *castellanus* means "like a castle." And, if you look closely at the tops of these clouds, you will notice that they look like castle turrets. Altocumulus castellanus clouds are mid-level clouds that can lead to thunderstorms. In fact, sometimes lightning will hop from one of these clouds to another.

altocumulus castellanus clouds

FUN FACT

Nacreous clouds are bright, rainbowlike, and extremely rare. These iridescent clouds can be found at high **latitudes** near the North and South Poles.

Weather Around the World

A view of Earth from space shows that our planet is covered in whirly, swirly clouds. In fact, NASA has stated that clouds typically cover over 65 percent of Earth's surface. Where these clouds appear on Earth may change, but no matter the time of year, over half of our planet is covered in clouds.

Viewing our planet through a wide lens is helpful when it comes to clouds. Using satellite pictures taken from space, scientists can see where clouds form most consistently. For example, regions near the **equator** are typically cloudy. This is because the equator receives direct sunlight throughout the year, causing temperatures to be high. Energy from the sun consistently heats the land, causing evaporation. This evaporation causes moist air to rise and condense, creating clouds.

During the Apollo 11 mission in 1969, astronauts took this picture of Earth from space.

air masses that affect North America

How large air masses move and interact affects where clouds form. Air masses blowing from tropical regions are often filled with warm air. Meanwhile, air masses blowing from polar regions are often filled with cold air. When air masses move, they bring the weather of where they came from with them. When air masses with different temperatures and moisture levels meet, they cause clouds—and storms.

arctic   polar   tropical

TECHNOLOGY

Weather Satellites

Weather satellites are designed to study cloud patterns, how clouds form, and how clouds travel. Meteorologists can make weather forecasts using data gathered from satellites. Forecasts can warn people when dangerous storms are on their way!

Severe Weather

Thunderstorms occur in three stages: developing stage, mature stage, and dissipating stage. During the developing stage, **currents** of warm air rise. This causes cumulus clouds to grow larger. Eventually, these clouds will develop into a single cumulonimbus cloud.

Next is the mature stage. At this stage, there are two types of air currents: warm and cold. Rising warm currents called *updrafts* continue to fuel the cloud. At the same time, downward-moving cold currents called *downdrafts* are descending from the cloud. Frozen water droplets begin to melt as they fall, causing rain. But if updrafts are strong enough, the frozen droplets don't have time to melt, and they fall to the ground as hail.

Finally, the storm enters its final stage, the dissipating stage. Downdrafts of cool air begin to overpower updrafts of warm air. In time, this causes a storm cloud to break up and disappear.

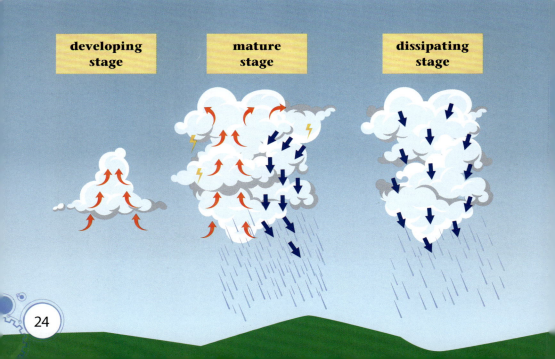

Thunderstorms can result in tornadoes, which are another type of storm. Tornadoes are formed when powerful updrafts create superfast, spinning pillars of air inside storm clouds. When these spinning pillars descend from storm clouds, they become devastating forces.

tornado

Giant thunderstorms that form over the ocean can develop into tropical storms. Tropical storms can develop into powerful hurricanes. These circular storms can be hundreds of kilometers wide and cause massive destruction. Hurricanes are fueled by warm, moist air, and they form over warm ocean water. Like thunderstorms, hurricanes dissipate when they lose access to updrafts.

hurricane

ENGINEERING

Civil Engineers

Civil engineers plan and design buildings and other structures so that they are strong enough to withstand large storms. Engineers build models of their structures and test them in different ways. They want to make sure that their structures stay standing during the fiercest winds and most powerful rain or hail.

Our Cloudy Planet

Clouds can be white, wispy, and delicate. They can be gray, massive, and thunderous, too! Clouds bring relief to parched land with rain. They also trap and reflect solar energy, helping humans stay cool *and* keep warm. Clouds can gather and build until they result in tropical storms and tornadoes. Such clouds are devastating forces of nature, leveling homes and flooding cities.

Earth's clouds take on many different forms, but they are composed of the same elements. Clouds are made up of millions of tiny water droplets, ice crystals, or both. Clouds are also caused by many forces. They are created through solar energy, the movement and interaction of air masses, and even the shapes of landforms. But cloud formation is always the same. It is caused by the rising, cooling, and condensing of moist air through the atmosphere.

thunderstorm in Bulgaria

We live on a cloudy planet, but ours isn't the only one. Clouds can be found on almost every planet in our solar system! Jupiter's clouds are yellow and made of ammonia. Mars's clouds are composed of water and carbon dioxide, and some of them shimmer with color. Venus's light-yellow clouds are made of sulfuric acid. Our study of clouds doesn't have to stop on our home planet. There is a whole universe of clouds to explore!

FUN FACT

Some exoplanets, which are planets outside of our solar system, may have clouds. Scientists have already found clouds on one exoplanet. NASA's James Webb Space Telescope examined an exoplanet named WASP-107b. Scientists detected clouds made of silicate, or sand!

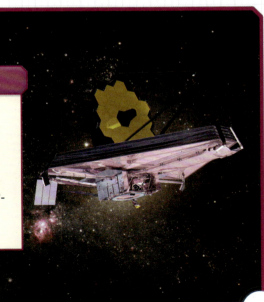

STEAM CHALLENGE

Define the Problem

Meteorologists have a challenging job. Not only do they have to predict weather based on probability, but much of what they interpret and conclude is based on instruments they use rather than what they can see. Meteorologists are looking for a visible model that demonstrates how air masses interact with one another. Your job is to provide them with a demonstration that proves how air masses flow within the atmosphere.

Constraints: You may only use the materials provided to you.

Criteria: Your model must use two liquids and should clearly and accurately demonstrate how areas of high and low atmospheric pressure interact.

Research and Brainstorm
What is an air mass? How do areas of high and low air pressure create weather patterns? How are temperature and humidity levels affected by air pressure? How can you create a visible model of an invisible phenomenon?

Design and Build
Sketch and label your idea, describing how your model will demonstrate air masses. Show how you can heat the materials, cool them, and combine them to demonstrate how different areas of pressure interact within our atmosphere. Collect the materials needed and build your model.

Test and Improve
Add food coloring to your two liquids. Begin by adding one colored liquid of your choice to your glass beaker. Write your observations and what air mass you believe this represents. Then, slowly and carefully, add your second colored liquid to top off the beaker. Write your observations and if there are any interactions between your air masses. Return to your research. Did your model clearly show how air pressures interact within the atmosphere? Make adjustments and test again.

Reflect and Share
What part of this challenge did you find the most interesting? If you could do this challenge again, what would you do differently? How does your model demonstrate an invisible phenomenon?

Glossary

air masses—large bodies of air that have consistent temperatures and amounts of moisture

air pressure—the total weight, or pressure, of the air around us

classifications—systematic arrangements in groups

cloud cover—a mass of clouds covering all or most of the sky

condenses—changes from a gas or vapor to a liquid

currents—bodies of air moving constantly in certain directions

dew—tiny drops of water that collect on the surfaces of cool objects at night

dissipate—to separate into parts and scatter or vanish

equator—imaginary line that divides Earth into the Northern Hemisphere and the Southern Hemisphere

fog—fine particles of water floating in the atmosphere near the ground

latitudes—distances north or south of the equator measured in degrees

meteorology—the study of Earth's atmosphere and weather

mist—water in the form of particles floating in the air or falling as fine rain

solar energy—energy created by the sun that produces heat

translucent—not transparent but clear enough to allow light to pass through

turbulence—irregular atmospheric motion with up-and-down currents of air

weather fronts—boundaries between two air masses that have different temperatures, winds, and amounts of moisture

weather satellites—human-made objects that circle Earth and study its weather and climate

Index

air masses, 11, 23, 26
air pressure, 4, 8–10
altitude, 8–9, 13–16
civil engineers, 25
Cloud Gate, 15
condensation, 4, 6–7, 9–11
condensation nuclei, 7
convergence, 10
evaporation, 4, 6, 10, 22
exoplanets, 27
fronts, 11, 19
high-level clouds, 16–17
Howard, Luke, 12, 16
hurricanes, 25

James Webb Space Telescope, 27
Kapoor, Anish, 15
low-level clouds, 16, 20
mid-level clouds, 16, 18, 21
rare clouds, 21
solar energy, 10, 26
thunderstorms, 21, 24–26
tornadoes, 5, 20, 21, 25–26
turbulence, 10
water vapor, 6, 9–10, 15, 17
weather satellites, 23

CAREER ADVICE
from Smithsonian

Do you want to be a meteorologist?
Here are some tips to keep in mind for the future.

"Use a weather app to compare cloud forecasts with what you actually see in the sky. It's an excellent way to develop your meteorology skills."

— *Dr. Natasha Hinojosa, Postdoctoral Researcher, Smithsonian Tropical Research Institute*

"Keep a cloud journal! Observe and sketch the clouds you see each day to learn about different types and weather patterns."

— *Dr. Aaron O'Dea, Staff Scientist, Smithsonian Tropical Research Institute*